The Landscape of Dreams

Margaret Fensom

The Landscape of Dreams

Acknowledgements

The following poems have been previously published:

'July Morning', *Friendly Street Reader* 36; 'Boxes', *Independent Weekly*, 14–20 July 2007; *Writers on Parade* Vol. 4:1; 'Empty House', *Muse* 236, February 2004; 'Haiku', *Haiku Bindii: Journeys* (1) ('Hot Summer Morning' also in *Writers on Parade* Vol. 2:1); 'Rain Blossoms', *The Starving Writers' Guide to Absolutely Everything*; 'Summer Night', *The Starving Writers' Guide to Absolutely Everything*; 'Autumn', *Writers on Parade*, Vol. 3:1; 'Alexander and the Rain', *Friendly Street Reader* 33; 'Visitor', *Writers on Parade*, Vol. 2:2; 'Black Cockatoos', *Writers on Parade*, Vol. 4:1; 'Bird Feet', *Writers on Parade*, Vol. 1:1; 'Carrickalinga', *The Starving Writers' Guide to Absolutely Everything Else*; 'Cyclist', *Writers on Parade*, Vol. 1:1; 'Old Woman Pruning', *Writers on Parade* Vol. 4:1; 'Hobbit Sam', *The Starving Writers' Guide to Absolutely Everything Else*; 'August 1945', *Writers on Parade*, Vol. 2:2; 'Wedding at Half Moon', *Writers on Parade*, Vol. 1:3; 'Contrail', *Friendly Street Reader* 23; 'Framboises', *Friendly Street New Poets* 12; 'Love Graffiti', *Writers on Parade*, Vol. 6; 'The Shoe that Went to Avignon', 'The Shoe that didn't go to Avignon', *Tamba* 46; 'Glenelg', *Writers on Parade*, Vol. 5; 'Moon Flowers', *Writers on Parade*, Vol. 4:1; 'Moon', *The Starving Writers' Guide to Absolutely Everything Else*; 'On leaving the House After a Hot Day', *Writers on Parade*, Vol. 5; 'Bee', *Tamba* 49; 'Greenhouse', *Friendly Street Reader* 15; 'Sea Dragon', *Writers on Parade*, Vol. 3:2; 'Silver Gull', *Tamba* 51; 'Voices', *Studio* 98

The Landscape of Dreams
ISBN 978 1 74027 895 9
Copyright © text Margaret Fensom 2014
Cover photo by the author, previously published in *Trains*

First published 2014
Reprinted 2016

GINNINDERRA PRESS
PO Box 3461 Port Adelaide SA 5015
www.ginninderrapress.com.au

Contents

July Morning	11
Boxes	12
Empty House	13
Haiku	14
Rain Blossoms	15
Park At Evening	16
Winter Is Just an Eye Blink	17
Rosella	18
Summer Night	19
Easter Trilogy	20
Autumn	22
Alexander and the Rain	23
Visitor	24
Black Cockatoos	25
Adelaide, City of Birds	26
Bird Feet	28
Carrickalinga	29
Cyclist	30
The Theft of Scent	31
Sheoaks	32
Squid	33
Old Woman Pruning	34
Hobbit Sam	35
Tabitha	36
August 1945	37
Wedding at Half Moon	38
Friday Evening – Rundle Mall	39
Contrail	40
Framboises	41
Rue des Abbesses, Paris	43

Half-moon Over Montmartre	44
Love Graffiti	45
The Shoe That Went To Avignon	46
The Shoe That Didn't Go To Avignon	47
Trans-Siberian: Vladivostok To Irkutsk	48
Lake Baikal	50
Borth	52
Aberdovey	54
Blaenau	55
SETI	56
Glenelg	57
Lament for Planet Earth	58
Moon Flowers	59
Moon	60
The Moon On My Prison	61
On Leaving the House After a Hot Day	62
Virtually Unseen	63
Sometimes	64
Bee	65
Greenhouse	66
Sea Dragon	67
Zebras Crossing	68
Silver Gull	69
Shadows and Light	70
Advent	71

Susan out of Narnia — 73

Nightfall	75
Magdalen College, Oxford	76
Voices	77
To Lucy, Queen of Narnia	78
Train to Nowhere	79
When You Went Away	80

Susan out of Narnia	81
Why	82
Aslan's Mane	83

The Landscape of Dreams

The country of dreams is near
to some place that you may know.
It has streets and houses you
may have seen
but its geography
doesn't quite add up.

The atlas of dreams
has pages
that are blank
or faded
around the edges.

The landscape of dreams is built
of places half-forgotten.
Its streets are formed
partly from remembered places but
its buses and trains roam far and do not
connect with routes you know.

The history of dreams contains
long walks never taken on roads
to forgotten country
tramlines where the sea almost foams
against their wheels
railway stations and old rural roads
that were never there
or maybe are reshaped
from old memories.

The country of dreams is
a place you may long to visit but
your feet will never take you and
there are no tickets you can buy.
Yet sometimes in the night
old places are revisited
in that tantalising glimpse
of times forgotten partly and
of things that never were.

July Morning

On this not-quite-frost morning
the native lilac
sprinkles its purple blooms
on the dry brush fence
plane tree leaves lie like cut-out paper stars
the sparse blades
of kangaroo grass are green in the sun
and plant shadows patch
the would-be lawn
recalling
black shadow lattice of the vine
bare in the full moon.

Boxes

Six years in this house
and already the dust has settled:
boxes still packed, whose contents are unknown,
under the bed papers of past campaigns –
poems piled like autumn leaves –

a trunk
where tissue paper wraps a white dress
in memory of silkworms
who died for my wedding.

Hidden under grey dust like ash
my past could be
like Pompeii unearthed.

Empty House

I return to the empty house.
It is not silent.

Something murmurs
and stops as I enter the door
as if some secret conversation from former lives
were interrupted by my presence

leaving
silence of sunny afternoon
thud of windows shaken by light breeze
birds pattering on the roof
a mute cat staring from large eyes
sound of cars
moving towards and away
away down the street

and in my ears
soft humming of motes.

Haiku

hot summer morning
I cross shadows
with a cyclist

gold sun dazzle
along shaded streets
rosellas fly

autumn leaf
a handprint
on the window

Japanese garden
even the butterflies
are bonsai

Rain Blossoms

In grey-green gum leaves
blossoms move like stars
across the curtain of night
and dark-eyed possums
squabble in moonlight.

Morning comes
and rainbow lorikeets
rend the cream-white blossoms
scatter bud caps.

Rainbows heedless of stars
fly screeching like green rain
and shatter the blue-glass morning with their cries.

Park At Evening

How strange is this place
where rosellas murmur beak to beak
hiding the colours you would not believe
had some painter brushed them onto canvas,
and the leaves are grey in dusk.

In an island of mud
lost in a sea of green grass.
a pale pink hibiscus flower
lies waiting for the evening star.

The horizon, colour of cut rock melon
turns lemon, fades.

Salmon-pink contrails spring out of nowhere
in the sky that girdles the whole earth.

Somewhere a Victorian house chimney
peers through the trees.

Winter Is Just an Eye Blink

It is only just July
and the white prunus flowers are come
presagers of little sour plums.
The pale narcissus stands in wintry gardens.
Two wood ducks graze together in the park.
Rosellas are pairing around tree hollows.
Soon the white-pink almonds
will bloom against stormy skies
and August thunder clouds
perhaps bring transient snow to the hills.
In this land
winter is just an eye blink.

Rosella

A rosella
jacaranda-feathered shoulders heaving
opens its dark blue wings
feathers edged with black
flying for fear of me.
Its back is the exquisite green
of new born leaves
head crimson and white –
O berries and roses.

The sky is blue and white
like wind-blown feather down
piling to lumps
of white curly wool.

There are those days of crystal blue,
days of rain
falling from blue-green leaves
and days of desert dust
when the bottlebrush
toss their red flowers against the sky
its blue hazing to summer heat.

Summer Night

Dusty dark sky
of summer
swings her chandelier
of golden stars.

Restless parrot flaps
to another tree.
Possums fight
in hall of leaf mirrors.

Easter Trilogy

Gethsemane

In that cold dark garden,
Paschal moon glitters
on dark olive leaves.

In Galilee bud
the lilies of the field.

Easter Eve

Autumn leaves glow like yellow wine
in this far country,
pale as the white sky darkens and the stars
glitter coldly.

Two thousand years and still we have not learned
to love,
still tear out eyes for eyes,
bloodily crush tooth for tooth.

And the universe
indifferently sweeps us
out to sea:
like ants.

Can we hope that the full moon
will bring resurrection?

Easter

Despair is old as our awareness
of hope.

But Mary Magdalene and her friends
did not need hope to go to the tomb.

And so it is told
from this and many other apparitions
that he lives
and as he lives, so shall we.

Autumn

It's autumn. We fold into ourselves.
And look, one morning the rain has arrived.
Stars peep between the whiteness of clouds.
Crickets sing in the late afternoon.

It isn't death we fear, nor mourn
shortness of life. As light grows soft
we fold ourselves into ourselves,
dream thoughts and sleepy slowness,
to find those depths we had forgotten,
strange dreams we never knew we had,
first green leaves of the bulbs
that bloom before winter's end,
tears at the cricket's sad fluting
in the early dusk.

Alexander and the Rain

Alexander, aged one,
sees the water falling from the clouds
silver grey onto the wooden table
turning red-brown in the rain,
sees the rain
deepen the red of paving bricks,
stretches out his little hand
to touch the water pools
forming under the drain pipe.

He has as yet
no words for colour.

Visitor

December cherries ripen red
in hills where yellow summer grass
is dry as smoke.

My vine bears grapes
hard and green.

Among jasmine flowers
and drying bottlebrush
my visitor, a tiny silver-eye,
still finds food.

Black Cockatoos

Soft cries
dark wings
down feather sky

Black cockatoos
seek pine nuts in their heavy cones
wheel over pine and gum
with welcome unfamiliar wings.

The cool west wind
echoes with their cries
as white vapour weaves
a shawl to catch the light.

Perhaps from the burned hills
those birds came years ago
like people fleeing war scorched lands.

Now under the blue white-clouded sky they come
as the hills are green with grass again, and valleys
below eucalypt-clad slopes are white
with hawthorn and lilies from a greener land.

Adelaide, City of Birds

Buongiorno's, Rundle Street*

On the gold-brown floor
a sparrow searches
under the wooden tables.
Its mate flies in
through the open front.
At three p.m. on a weekday
the place is almost empty
except for sparrows.

Lorikeets

In a white-flowered gum
rainbow lorikeets
screech at their nectar feast.
Night comes and blossoms move
softly in wind swaying like
a curtain of stars
falling falling
like snow.

Torrens Building, Victoria Square

On stone ledges
cut from mountains
lorikeets lodge
with pigeons.

Norwood Street

Rosellas flying out
of the big gums in the park
pause in the dry winter-leaved plane tree
to pick plane tree balls.
I remember
rosellas with liquidambar pods
round and spiky like strange stars.

In my garden

Pinstriped wattle bird
drinks from orange tecoma flowers.
Despising fading pink gum blossoms
a tiny spinebill
probes yellow jessamine.

They say that rats desert
a sinking ship.

And birds?
They have not left us…yet.

---

* The site of the former Buongiorno's Caffe, Rundle Street, is now occupied by Caffe Brunelli.

Bird Feet

Dark and lovely
is the trine foot*
of a bird
scratching pit-pat
on the roof,
three black tines shadowing through
translucent veranda
dusted with vine debris.

For the world is criss-crossed
by bird feet
fading into the future
haunting memory.

May such feet
ever imprint
this place.

---

* Birds have three toes in front on which they walk and a fourth claw, or spur, coming out from the back of the foot higher up.

Carrickalinga

Sage-green and khaki sea
sweeps layer on white-edged layer
to Carrickalinga sands.

Amber-green sea grapes
embroider foam lines.
Weed spray lies like stranded lizard.

Broken basalt rises
sudden in sea-edge sands.

On the pale dunes
dark-leaved gazanias
spring out of black decay:
orange flowers flame.

Tussock grass fans
straw mingled with green
bright russet streaks
streaming away from the wind.

Blue-green coarse runner grass
clasps the sea spray dunes
before they drift away like white smoke
and the black bones of the sea are laid bare.

Cyclist

rain cloak
red gleaming wet at twilight
flies on cobweb spokes
under the moon

The Theft of Scent

I don't take other people's flowers.
I steal their perfume with my breath.
I brush my hands along the leaves
of lavender and rosemary.
Ah, surely this is not a crime.

Sheoaks

Seeming unlovely, spike-leaved,
without the sheen of pine needles
romance of cypress columns
against straw covered hills,
sheoaks bud
with the grace of sea urchins
spike-clustered like exploding stars,
spread netted leaves
against the pale sky,
sing with their dark leaves
in desert wind.

Squid

Huge eyes
love ballet in the crushing deeps
pale streamers fragile-seeming in dark
silk sea of adamantine force

Other minds
that rise to moonlight
and dive
naked to darkness
where we
follow in sea-depth space ships

How can we know
if the deep sea delights
or is just the street
where instinct walks
and hunger and terror flash
for a moment
into dark minds?

Old Woman Pruning

White jasmine yields its perfume to the shears.
Wisteria keeps its place.

She knows
all things are not now possible.

But still
red rose petals
spill
lawless into the courtyard.

A blackbird sings.

Hobbit Sam

I'm not really human, said Sam.
I'm a hobbit.

My ancestor was Samwise
who saw elves

helped his master destroy some ring or other.

I don't remember, but I'm sure it was important.

I'm not interested in ancient history.
I just go on and on
growing gardens in secret corners.

Without them the world would be dark.

Tabitha

Tabitha sits silken
like a lion in the grass.
White moon rises
Sun shadows stretch.

Green eyes close.
The pale throat is turned to the moon.
Lids, like a mask, are lined with black.

Bird shadows flutter
in ghostly leaves
deceiving tips of lizards' tails
grey butterflies of memory*
woven in nets of reverie.

After summer moonrise
old Tabitha dreams.

---

* Cats are capable of seeing colour but movement is more important to them.

August 1945

A photo stirs
an early memory:
my mother, aunt, two cousins,
myself with light brown hair,
just two years old
on a beach in southern England.

Our war was over.

In Hiroshima
toddlers innocent as I
at Ground Zero.

Wedding at Half Moon

There go the married people (just),
three white Chevys scouring the road
with full throttled roar.

May the white half-moon
shine gently on you.

Friday Evening – Rundle Mall

White burning sun
shines the pavement
her hair mingling with city dust
throws into bas-relief cigarette butts
hopes dreams indifference
long hurrying shadows.

Someone holds up a *Big Issue* for the sun to read
or those who pass.
Light blurs its pages
seller ignored.

Excited sparrows roost in the dark leaves
of a small tree.

People pack up the Amnesty candle stand.

I hurry past to catch a train
cannot stop.

Hanky falls from azure silk sleeve
more debris
as the setting sun
ripens like a large pink fruit.

Contrail

Flame without candle
the contrail comes
out of a sky marbled with clouds
where the gold sun slipped
behind the rim of the world

spark at its head
laden with souls
white down feather
trailing burnished vapour
insect caught in evening's gold
fleeing sunset into night.

Once I too sailed in such a frail craft
watching the grey blue river
as dawn rose over Budapest.

But I fled westwards
and the sun pursued.

Framboises

Framboises, rich red raspberries
ten francs a punnet

and I who have battled
the SNCF –
also the Irish ferry company
whose people only speak French
trying to book a passage to Ireland –
I love this city, Paris, but must leave –

climb the long stairs from the Metro
past birch forest mural with pink flowers –
faint fringe of spring,
walk past open shop fronts
see them
rich red raspberries.
How can I resist?

In my room on the sixth floor
(no lift)
I eat them all,
gaze from my balcony in the roof
at the white apartments opposite
pale shutters and geranium window boxes
blooms on the balcony.

One apartment is *à vendre*

(had I but wealth enough and time)

Somehow I feel at home in these streets
where people speak another language,
but for me
no fine French cooking could compare
with tart sweet ruby-red fresh raspberries.

Rue des Abbesses, Paris

When I returned to the rue Abbesses
after nine years, I had another room.
It looked out over red tiled roofs and washing lines,
not the white walls and elegant façade
of the apartments opposite.
But from the street I saw them, paint a little worn.
The pink blooms on the balcony were gone,
nor did I see geraniums in window boxes
that August, but unseen, up the hill
was the white dome of Sacré Coeur,
all lit inside with candles
for evening adoration.

Perhaps one day in winter
I will make one last trip (or more)
and the black iron balconies and folded shutters
will be dusted with snow
and Sacré Coeur
gleam pale against a wintry sky,
the full moon shining
over a city all black and white and window gold.

And I will stand again on my small balcony
and put my hand upon the sloping roof,
and I will leave my print on whiteness
as the full moon shines on Paris under snow.

Half-moon Over Montmartre

Paris is hazy as usual.
Half-moon hangs
like red balloon part seen
in smoky misty sky.

Far below
Paris laid out in pastel squares
shows dreams of artists are real.

You can see the grey slate roofs
where windows with balconies look out
over pale apartments and geranium window boxes
like the room that is mine for three days.

It would seem that all the world is seated
on the steps of Sacré Coeur
with the white domes and the copper knights turned green
if I had not seen the crowds
in streets nearby and in the artists' square.

A young man sings to music of soft drums.
Someone plays a flute.
The young applaud.

I pause.
The air is cool
after a long summer day.

The Ferris wheel
in Tuileries garden slows and stops.
Les Invalides' dome
is dull gold in the dusk.

Half-moon over Montmartre

Love Graffiti

Botanical Gardens Adelaide

White messages of love
encrypted
on the green bark of bamboo

but who knows
as stem grows and swells
what hearts will be broken
loves forgot

and who
loving still will bring
their young child to walk in this park.

The Shoe That Went To Avignon

I find I am wearing odd shoes.

One, with a hole in the toe,
walked, but did not dance, on the Bridge at Avignon –
oh, those cobblestones.
(But long ago they danced
sous not *sur le pont*
in a café under the bridge.)
The other has never travelled overseas
and is now too old
to take on holiday.

But, returning to Avignon, I recall
walking inside the city wall
over cobblestones in thin-soled shoes
under a blazing August sun,
looking for the famous bridge,
then though an ancient archway
along beside the river.

And there, in the distance one-third of a bridge,
monument to the vision
of Bénezet, a simple shepherd boy,
reached part way into the blue-green Rhone,
a dream marooned in time
yet still living.

Shoes return home, leather worn,
lie in silver dust under beds.

But they have walked the dream of rivers crossed,
ancient as faith, new as sunrise each morning.

The Shoe That Didn't Go To Avignon

No, I never walked
on the bridge at Avignon
nor saw the empty palace of the French Popes,

but we all travelled
in cardboard boxes after being made
by people who cannot afford
to travel to Europe.

And I have walked
by secret pools of water
and green hanging leaves
under the red walls
of the ancient rock sacred
to a people far older
than those who built the bridge at Avignon.

I have seen the desert flowers,
walked in the green parks
at the sea's edge in Darwin.

We all come to resting in the end:
kicked out of sight for tidiness,
companions to frightened cats.

Trans-Siberian: Vladivostok To Irkutsk

Music plays.
The train begins to move:

wooden houses
tin roofs
silver summer sea.

No snow waste,
orange and yellow lilies:
summer fields Siberia.

Evening falls;
people with sticks
drive cows and goats.

Brown wooden huts
under quiet hills:

wood stacked up for winter,
potato field,
cow on common.

Warm white nights,
tiger far away.

In my dreams he stalks
pale dark striped
under stars.

Sand by pale water
clouds reflected:
Lake Baikal.

Irkutsk:
wooden houses
trams in the rain.

Mountains
water forget-me-not blue;
remember winter ice.

Deep in the lake
over long ages
the continent divides.

My small feet
touch icy water:
edge of ocean birth.

Lake Baikal

I take off my shoes and stand
ankle deep
in icy water.
Lake Baikal
the deepest fresh water
lake on earth
is where they say
Eurasia divides.

Ocean embryo
how fearful are the deep waters
yet
folklore says
my brief immersion has gained me
another year of life beyond my span.

At the edge of this mystery
a longing
for immortality
rises.

I want to see this ocean
the new divided continents.

Yet what sorrows
the years may bring:
loss of what is held dear
the face of the earth
wholly changed.

If (as I believe) there is a God
who confers immortality
He who is also She and neither will transform
us into creatures who can bear
the burden of the ages, knowing the end.

But for us mortals
our longing
is tinged with trepidation.

Borth

So I went to Borth
ancestral village in the mother line:
grey flat Borth
where the train lines
coming through the mountains
from Shrewsbury
Machynlleth
or north from Aberystwyth
meet in the fields at Dovey Junction:
curlicues
of water in the marshy ground.

I walk the sea wall
by the sandy beach
the town strung out almost a single street
along the flat places,
and up into the hills:
Upper Borth they say.

They say with rising sea
Borth will disappear
Perhaps the mountains higher will loom
over Borth beneath the sea.
No Atlantis
just a disused small port.

I returned years later and the grey
terrace houses
on the road to the railway station
were brightly painted.
Borth had become a rainbow-coloured town.
But still the gulls
wheeled and wailed over the sea wall;
still the railway platform
looked out over grazing sheep
and St Matthew's on a mound in the fields.

Aberdovey

There are flowers on the platform at Aberdovey
the little station between two tunnels.
Northwards the train runs
between the mountains and the sea,
sheep on the slopes hemmed in
by the hard lace of limestone walls,
wide estuaries
covered by sand at low tide
pale blue grey sea stretching wide
when the tide is high.
Taller the mountains march inland.
We bypass Porthmadog where the steam train
leaves for Blaenau Ffestiniog.
Another time
I take the steam train from Minnffordd
to the slate mountains,
but following the coast the train runs
past Harlech Castle
to Pwllheli
where I sit on the sand with sandwiches
wade in crystal-clear water.
Mist
lies on the sea and throws
a light veil over
the three-storey terraces fronting the beach.

Blaenau

Broken viaduct
slate mountain
in shadow.
Slice of sun
shines on white-walled cottages.

SETI*

In the land
of coloured birds
purple hills from which the snows
had lately melted never to return
star like creatures
in ocean's green depths
perishing
summer too warm
winter kind of nice
but no rain no crops
the people of radio land
searched the stars:
We are surely not alone
what if this blue gem
of a planet
rolls on silent
without us
without the singing birds
not wholly lifeless but bereft
of all music and creatures we can love
before we find anyone at all?

As he watched the last block
of his pyramid placed
in perfect alignment with the stars
the pharaoh had no idea
the aliens were looking for him.

---

* Search for extra-terrestrial intelligence by looking for non-natural patterns of radio waves

Glenelg

Moseley Square, December 2009

At nine o'clock in the evening
land parched on a warming planet
the sea gleams like blue ink.

Quick red feet of gulls
scurry across the paving.

The palm tree leaves are drying
as sunset's tangerine glow
fades from the horizon.

Jupiter shines in the west
pale pearl cradled
in the deep blue shell of evening.

Lament for Planet Earth

Dusky blue sky of twilight
speaks peace as the sun withdraws its warmth
and the earth takes of deep breath.

The moon is as fine as the edge
of a pear-blossom petal,
though she grows nightly,

shines through the coloured glass
of my window on the sky
and sparkles silver through
the rippled glass.
So am I blest while the world wilts.

She watches the white ice glaciers,
white mountain tops become bare rock,
the rivers that fed millions dry.
The snow geese fail
and polar bears become a legend
rumour of bones beneath the sea.

But she, pale witness of our warming,
remembers no bird song,
nor has the rustle of leaves
ever disturbed her barren sands.

In green shade
I see grapes colour of chrysoprase
hang from the abundant vine;
birds drink from orange flowers.

Too late, we see our Eden as it fails;
even the thorns and briars are sweet remembrances.

Moon Flowers

On the moon
there are no flowers
in its fine silver dust
that shines back to us from the sky.
There are vast mountains
but no running streams
no singing birds no trees.

But in its long night
the stars must be brilliant
and in its heavens gleams
the pale blue orb of Earth.

Moon

The moon
orange as sunflower
is clutched by charcoal cloud.

A spark glows on its horn
as it glides below darkness to its setting.

The Moon On My Prison

The moon glittered on the mountains
of Afghanistan.

The moon glittered on the sea
the dark sea
as we sailed over sharks,
huddled in our leaking boat.

The moon glittered over razor wire
as we waited,
and I grew.

The moon glittered on the leaves
of this they called the Land of Freedom;
but we were not free.

Now at last I am free.

But last night the moon did not shine
over an Island called Christmas
where others sought freedom

and were dashed on the rocks.

Their freedom is beyond this world.

On Leaving the House After a Hot Day

The house is a monster.
Its walls breathe heat.
I leave one window open for the cat,
a timid guard, but one with feisty teeth
she won't use on a burglar,
just on me.

Virtually Unseen

Down there in the virtual mud
at the roots of the long grass
on my computer screen
there are perhaps frogs
crickets who sing
while shadows lengthen
over the hills
but I will never see them.

My words perhaps outlive my life
in that cyberspace,
but never will those frogs
be heard, or leap out of their ditch.

Outside my window
are yellowing leaves
orange flowers
and noisy birds.
These I see and hear.

Night creeps across the pale sky.

Sometimes

Sometimes I get lost among the leaves
where songbirds become dragons
and the black cat doubt
holds the diamond understanding
in its fearsome paw.

Sometimes the sky is milk dreams
Summer a grey haze
White butterfly the mind drifts.

Bee

The white flower to the virgin bee,
'Come, take my sweetness and make
me fruitful.'

The golden load
of pollen
is carried by lives ephemeral
in sun and flower
yielding the dark sweet honey
to the white wax cell,

that see by eyes multiform
colours and the angle of the sun
dance to show
the long flight path to sweetness

no life except the hive and those
long voyages
reading the light.*

---

* Bees can see polarisation of light and use it to locate nectar sources, the location of which is shown by dances in the hive.

Greenhouse

Man,
Man is too clever by half.
When he acquired the knowledge of good and evil
you might have thought he would put it to better use.

First he keeps out the winter by warming his home –
and the whole earth – by three or four degrees.
The water rises, the crops fail.
Then he makes a hole in the ozone
and scorches himself.

If he doesn't blow himself up, he'll make famines
by cutting down all the trees.

He can't seem to get it right
(and neither can she).

Sea Dragon

Forget-me-not silk ribbon of sea
lies between the edge of our habitation
and the sky.

On its margins lies the shadow
of amber forests gleaming.

Here be dragons
tiny fragile dragons
that live among the forests of the sea.

Under the shining salt waves curl
the slender tails of dragon steeds
round amber-green frilled weed
above the reef where living shells and stars
move secretly beneath the sea.

A dark cloud shape stalks the shore
as our world seeps into theirs.

Zebras Crossing

Zebras cross,
taut calves over slender ankles,
balanced on high heels,
or sloppy boots,
thick bare legs under sensible skirts.

Zebras cross
in blue jeans
and tailored trousers
creases undulating as they cross
in the rain
in the wind
as the lions wait
pale auto eyes aflame at twilight.

Zebras have
small slender necks and sharp cut hair,
little foal legs in pink tights
too-long jeans on baby colt legs
snow white or navy running shoes.

The lions wait obedient
as the zebras carry
bags, orange as mandarins,
blue as the dawn sky,
crusty bread peeping out
among carrots and beans
new zebra coats and pretty things
sparkling glass mane ornaments.

Their hooves flash by in twilight:
and the lions wait.

Silver Gull

Sun shines low beneath
white underwings
as she wheels in to land
runs with her scarlet legs
along the crystal mirror
of sea edge sand
where the frilled wave
has just retreated
waits for the next tiny wave
scooping with her blood-red beak
that lately ravished
a fish from its watery home
runs on the sand
squabbling for scraps
merciless
to the brown-legged dapple-winged young.

Her stone-white eyes
seem to hold no love
but of late
she brooded her chicks
in her nest among the sand bushes
fed them from her crop
fish from the grey-green sea.

Shadows and Light

'God is light and in him is no darkness at all' – 1 John 1:5

But God also made shadows.

Dark over water
tree shadow lies.
Forests green hold shadows
like cathedrals where light falls silent
on sacred stone.
Moths move in shadow
with their white wings.

Shadows in sunlight pattern the ground,
tracing the forms of trees and flowers.
Grass shadows trail their nets in the field,
and small leaf shadows, passing through my window,
move on the wall, as the sun falls.

Butterfly wings move over grass.
Their shadows passing make holes in sunlight
till its departure shows
in deeps of space
the meadows of the stars.

Advent

Sunset red as fire fades to grey
leaf patterns dark against the sky
world of incredible beauty,
pain unbearable.
We who weep for lost forms
patterns of beauty lost, vanished loves, mourn.

Did he come to this transient world to undo
the Gordian knot of time and death that all
forms of stardust
might live again?

Susan out of Narnia

The supposed later life and spiritual journey of Susan, one of the original four children who visited Narnia in C.S. Lewis's Chronicles of Narnia, after her brothers and sister entered the heavenly Narnia.

Nightfall

Night is falling
but the path outside
is a road of gold
and the leaves are honey.

Surely evening is not the end of day,
says Clive Staples Lewis.
The world is ugly
the world is cruel.

Surely there is a place
where children can escape the land of shadows
for a while.
Those who believe shall see.

Magdalen College, Oxford

Stone arches guard
green quadrangle
where strangers cannot tread.

Among the queens and bishops stand the beasts:
talking beasts of Narnia
satyr bishop and lion
crowned heads
stand silent in the sun.

Shadows fall upon stone
dew of evening on the grass.
Children unseen
slip into Narnia
and solemnly the beasts follow them.

Voices

Voices
voices of children,
those who wandered
out of the world's sunlight
to Narnia, land of dreams.

Dreams come to me
dreams in the darkness.
Children are kings and queens.
That world was fairer
than any I have known

But I escaped.
I alone am living
under the shadow of this weary sun.

To Lucy, Queen of Narnia

Once you and I were queens
among the talking beasts
wild hills of Narnia
palaces of gold
pavilions
among the apple trees.

But I dream.
You were little more than a child
when you left us.

It is I who have lived.

Maybe…maybe
we will meet again in Narnia.

Train to Nowhere

This train leads nowhere, Susan said
only to darkness.
I am left alone in the light of this world
and there is no other.

Oh my father, Oh my mother
Oh Peter, Edmund, Lucy.
You took the train to darkness
and left me all alone.

When You Went Away

When you went away
horror and darkness shrouded me.
I never dreamed that such a day as this
could dawn for me.
This Narnia, it was a dew
of innocence that vanishes
when the sun wakens flowers to its warmth.
But you were laid in earth
for love of Narnia you sought.

I have covered myself with flowers
in imitation of your graves.
I have cherished red silk
as a beacon to burn up grief,
savoured the fruits of the earth
to feed the emptiness of my soul,
laid fingers in silver filigree
seeking to know the workmanship of God.

But sometimes in the city
I think I hear his roar,
or in the woodlands think to see
a glimpse of Aslan:
empty silence
rustling of dry leaves.

Susan out of Narnia

Last night I saw Aslan
in the window of an empty church.

Many sorrows have covered me
and joys too, dancing joys,
since last I saw his golden mane
in the dreamland Narnia.

I was a queen, kings wooed me
but I thought it childish dream.
I have known real joys
childbed and marriage bed:
no phantoms these.
My children live and breathe.

I remember that day
the train wreck that ended my youth:
Peter, Edmund, Lucy
crushed bodies laid in earth
Mother and Father too.
Their foolish dream betrayed them.
Or so I thought…but now…

I am old…what hope for me?
Can I too enter heavenly Narnia?

Why

When I look and see
the torment of the world
I know, I think,
why Aslan left me here.

But my butterfly hands
brush vainly against
the falling leaves of the world.

My prayers flutter in the wind
not as the joyful prayer flags
of an older faith
just whispers in dry air.

Aslan's Mane

I have seen
the invisible mane of Aslan in the stars
his breath in the milky way
his eyes in the eyes of his children.

His paws walk through the forest.
His eyes weep
for all oppressed upon earth.
His ears hear music and all sighs.
His roar is in the voice of poets,
in the sound of anguished prayers.

www.ingramcontent.com/pod-product-compliance
Lightning Source LLC
Chambersburg PA
CBHW062146100526
44589CB00014B/1708